Gallery Books
Editor: Peter Fallon

THE BACCHAE

Derek Mahon

THE
BACCHAE

after Euripides

Gallery Books

The Bacchae
is first published
simultaneously in paperback
and in a clothbound edition
on 26 August 1991.

The Gallery Press
Loughcrew
Oldcastle
County Meath
Ireland

ISBN 1 85235 067 9 (*paperback*)
    1 85235 068 7 (*clothbound*)

The Gallery Press receives financial assistance from An Chomhairle Ealaíon / The Arts Council, Ireland, and acknowledges also the assistance of the Arts Council of Northern Ireland in the publication of this book.

for Patricia King

Only so much of the Dionysian sub-stratum of the universe may enter an individual consciousness as can be dealt with by the Apollonian transfiguration; so that these two prime agencies must develop in strict proportion and in accordance with the principles of eternal justice. Whenever the Dionysian forces become too obstreperous, as is the case today, we are safe in assuming that Apollo is close at hand, though wrapped in a cloud, and that the rich effects of his beauty will be witnessed by a later generation.

— F. W. Nietzsche, *The Birth of Tragedy*

I have tried to show that Euripides' description of Maenadism is not to be accounted for in terms of the imagination alone; that inscriptional evidence reveals a closer relationship with actual cult than scholars have realized; and that the Maenad, however mythical certain of her acts, is not in essence a mythological character but an observed and still observable human type. Dionysus still has his votaries or victims, though we call them by other names; and Pentheus was confronted by a problem which other civil authorities have had to face in real life.

— E. R. Dodds, *The Greeks and the Irrational*

Yeats's efflorescence in old age is perhaps unique in recent poetry. We might compare Euripides who, after a long life spent in struggling with and digesting new ideas, in gradually formulating a sceptical, rationalist attitude, had in his old age the elasticity to admit that there was a case for Dionysus.

— Louis MacNeice, *The Poetry of W. B. Yeats*

Characters

DIONYSUS
PENTHEUS
CADMUS
TIRESIAS
HERDSMAN
SOLDIERS
AGAVE
BACCHAE
CHORUS OF ASIAN WOMEN

For a description of Bacchic dance, see Dodds, Appendix 1, 'Maenadism'.

Notes on pronunciation

Dionysus. Zeus. Semele. Cadmus. Hera. Bacchae. Agave: Agaavay. Pentheus. Bacchant. Cithaeron. Corybantes. Rhea. Tiresias. Ino: Eeno. Autonoe: Autonoway. Lydian: Liddian. Bacchantes. Demeter: Demeeter. Delphi: Delphy. Actaeon. Artemis. Pieria: Pee-airia. Hubris: hyoobris. Tmolus. Echion. Orpheus. Maenad: Meenad. Asopus. Hysiae: Heesi-eye. Erythrae: Erith-reye. Aristaeus: Arist-ayus.

ACT ONE

Before the palace at Thebes; morning. A perpetual flame on Semele's tomb downstage. Empty wine-skins scattered about. Lights up on DIONYSUS, *a gaily dressed young man, his hair long and curly, a thyrsus in one hand. He wears a fawnskin and sandals, moves blithely, and speaks in a light, gay voice. The fawnskin is a decorative scarf, the thyrsus a fennel wand wreathed with ivy.*

DIONYSUS

My name is Dionysus, son of Zeus
and Semele, Cadmus' eldest daughter. Whoosh!
I was delivered by a lightning-flash
and here I am back home in Thebes again
pretending to be a mortal among men
although, as we all know, I am one of the gods.
Over there, in the corner, a monument records
my mother's death by lightning. She lived here
till — pow! — the place was blown to bits by Hera,
the jealous bitch. But Cadmus keeps it nice,
his daughter's and my mother's sacred place.
I've just been decorating it with vines . . .
I spent years on the hot Iranian plains,
in Saudi deserts and in Indian ports
where the sun shines indiscriminately on all sorts.
It was out there, in what we call the East,
that I began my Dionysian quest,
evolved my rites and, incidentally,
picked up the Chorus you'll meet presently.
Why did I choose Thebes as the first place
to do my Dionysian stuff in Greece?
I'll tell you. Mother's sisters claimed that I

was not the son of Zeus; that Semele
(pregnant, they said, by some mere mortal man)
got the idea from Cadmus, made it known
that Zeus was my *real* father; and this sin
was the reason Zeus' wife Hera did her in.
                    (*coughs apologetically*)
I'm afraid I've driven those aunties round the bend.
They've left their homes in town and gone to spend
their days among the mountains, where they wave
                    (*demonstrates*)
the Dionysian thyrsus, rant and rave.
Not only Cadmus' daughters, but virtually the whole
feminine population rock 'n' roll
among the rocks, under the moonlit pines;
                    (*severely*)
for Thebes must learn my purpose, which remains
a mystery to her citizens; and I
must vindicate my mother Semele
by demonstrating in this sceptical place
that I am a true son of the god Zeus.
The Bacchae roam the mountains by the dozen.
Cadmus, meanwhile, has given up his throne
to Agave's son Pentheus, his grandson —
Agave, one of those aunts I mentioned earlier on;
so Pentheus, a king but not a god, is my own cousin.
Pentheus, a rational, pretentious man,
refuses to acknowledge who I am,
denies the godhead I shall demonstrate
to him and all the people of this state.
Having achieved that, I shall travel on
                    (*smiles*)
to some equally fortunate dominion.
Meanwhile, should Pentheus frustrate my plan
and try to force the Bacchae home again,
there will be war between the Bacchant wives
and the strict spirit that controls their lives.
                    (*music off*)
Now, that will be my Chorus that you hear,
women who've followed me from the East and share
my own objectives.

12

> *(shouts)*
> Right, now, pipe and drum!
> Let Thebes know Dionysus, son of Semele, is come!
> *(suavely)*
> Excuse me, I must join the Bacchic dames
> on Mount Cithaeron where they play their games.

> *Winks and exit. Enter a* CHORUS *of Asian women with
> pipes, drums, and tambourines, dressed in Anatolian
> gipsy fashion, very colourful and striking. They dance
> and fall silent. When they speak their instruments are
> silent and they address the audience directly, one at a
> time, except during musical interludes, because music
> drowns out the words and we have to hear the words,
> please. The music should vary greatly, from a reflective
> mode to hard rock, according to the mood of the
> moment.*

CHORUS
> Over the sea from Asia
> we follow our Bacchic lord;
> night and day are a pleasure
> thanks to the laughing god.
> Let nobody interfere,
> shut your houses tight;
> Dionysus' women are here
> to give you all a fright!

> *Music and dance.*

> Happiness lies in a proper respect for the gods —
> for *all* the gods, the moderate and the fierce.
> You can make a cult of mystical solitudes,
> of self-denial and worse;
> but happy the man or woman
> who, to be truly human,
> respects the ivied thyrsus
> and worships it in honour of Dionysus.
> Pipe and drum, pipe and drum;
> let Thebes know Dionysus, son of Semele, is come!

13

Music and dance.

When Hera's lightning-flash
struck Semele in the womb
she died, but her son was born
and hidden safe by Zeus
until the day came round
when Dionysus might be seen and known.
Pipe and drum, pipe and drum;
let Thebes know Dionysus, son of Semele, is come!

Music and dance.

Thebes, the home of Semele,
will soon be hung with ivy,
with vine-leaves and wild roses,
its thoroughfares and houses
decorated in honour of Dionysus.
Soon, when he wishes it,
Thebes itself will quit
its ordered life and dance into the hills,
its citizens remembering
as they dance and sing
how in the Cretan glade
where Zeus was born, wild Corybantes played
the pipe and drum, and Rhea found
great satisfaction in the sound.
Great mother Rhea,
music and dance were your idea;
be here in spirit in the coming crisis,
mother of Zeus, grandmother of Dionysus.
Pipe and drum, pipe and drum;
let Thebes know Dionysus, son of Semele, is come!

Music and dance.

Raise your eyes to the hills
where, clad only in skins, the lord
of the dance wrestles the goat and kills
it, eats it raw and drinks its blood.

The Bacchae scream with delight,
the rivers are turned to wine
while Dionysus leads the dance
and shakes his hair in the wind.
This will go on all night,
we've seen it many a time,
everyone there in a trance
induced by the music's sound.
Pipe and drum, pipe and drum;
let Thebes know Dionysus, the lord of the dance, is come!

*Music and dance; then enter blind Tiresias. He wears a
fawnskin and knocks the palace door with his stick,
ivy-wreathed like a thyrsus.*

TIRESIAS
(*calls*)
Anyone there? I want to speak to Cadmus, please,
my great friend and the man who founded Thebes;
Tiresias is here, tell the old fool.
(*to audience*)
I'm old myself, of course, but he's older still.
We agreed to get ourselves some Bacchic gear
(*indicates his fawnskin*)
and go to the famous *céilí*, like half the women here.

Enter Cadmus, similarly got up.

CADMUS
Tiresias, old chap, I *thought* I heard you shout.
You're looking pretty dashing, I must say.
It suits you, makes a change. I'm kitted out,
as the young god insists, in the same way —
a fawnskin scarf, an ivied fennel rod . . .
Do you think my grandson is a real live god?
Where do we go, do you know? I could dance
all night, and all day too, given half a chance.
(*demonstrates with a jig*)
What do you say, shall we be young men once more?

TIRESIAS
(*giggles*)
You're as young as you feel; they're all in the hills up there.

CADMUS
(*anxiously*)
Do you think perhaps we ought to take a car?

TIRESIAS
No, that would be disrespectful; better go as we are.

CADMUS
You're right, we'll walk; it's really not that far.
Give me your hand and let's be going, so.
I'm a religious man at heart, you know.

They start to exit.

TIRESIAS
I can't abide our rational theology;
the old beliefs are good enough for me.
Sophisticated re-interpretations
will never interfere with *my* devotions.
The anti-Bacchic crowd will say that we're
undignified to join the dance up there;
but no, young Dionysus will be pleased
to see *age* represented at his feast.

CADMUS
(*glances off*)
Tiresias, don't look now, but the young king,
my grandson, Pentheus, is hurrying
in our direction, and he seems put out.
Wait till we see what this is all about.

*Enter PENTHEUS, a severe young man, and SOLDIERS.
At first he doesn't notice CADMUS, TIRESIAS or the
CHORUS.*

CADMUS
(*continues*)
Oh dear, he looks as if he'd like to break
somebody's neck for them!

PENTHEUS
(*kicks the empty wine-skins impatiently*)
                                        Oh, for fuck's sake!
(*to the audience*)
I've been abroad, where I heard strange reports
of scandalous goings-on back here in Thebes —
women leaving their homes on some pretext
of a Bacchic cult, making fools of themselves
in the woods and mountains, dancing indecently
in honour of Dionysus, a self-styled god.
There's drinking going on there, I've been told,
and sexual licence of the vilest kind;
and this, they claim, is a religious rite.
I call it some kind of hysteria.
Some of them are confined here in the town;
as for the others, I shall hunt them down,
and that includes my own mother Agave,
Ino, Autonoë . . . . Once I have them fast
I'll knock some sense into their silly heads.
I hear too that some Oriental quack,
a Lydian magician if you please,
with golden ringlets, his face flushed with wine,
brimful of charm and mischief, is in town,
consorting shamelessly with innocent girls,
luring them on with Bacchic mysteries.
Wait till I get my hands on him, I'll tear
the head clean from his shoulders; then we'll see
about those golden locks and flashing eyes!
This is the one who claims that Dionysus is a god,
that he was sewn up in the thigh of Zeus
when the fact is, of course, that Dionysus never lived,
destroyed by lightning in his mother's womb,
both struck down in a flash because the silly woman
claimed to have slept with Zeus himself. Whoever
this undesirable foreigner may be,

hanging's too good for him, it seems to me.

> PENTHEUS, *turning to leave, sees* CADMUS *and*
> TIRESIAS. *Sarcastically.*

Another mystery! Tiresias
and my own grandfather, Bacchantes both,
in hides, no less, the thyrsus in their hands!
You'd think men of your age would have more sense
than to appear in such a grotesque guise.
Grandfather, ditch that garland, if you please,
and rid yourself of that ridiculous wand.
You put him up to this, Tiresias!
By introducing a new god you expect
to do more business and collect more fees
inspecting entrails; but I tell you straight,
were it not for your white hair I'd have you put
in prison with the Bacchae for encouraging
pernicious practices. This isn't worship.
What do you think they're *up* to in the mountains?
The whole thing's an excuse for drink and sex.

> CHORUS

Sir, this is blasphemy. Revere the gods
and Cadmus too, who sowed the dragon-seed
your father sprang from. You disgrace your breed.

> PENTHEUS *stares at the* CHORUS *for the first time,*
> *in amazement and contempt.*

> TIRESIAS
> (*to* PENTHEUS)

If a wise man has something important to say
eloquence follows as the night the day.
You have the quick tongue of a politician
yet you are ignorant. A forceful man
with power and rhetoric at his finger-tips,
but without wisdom, can destroy the state.
You sneer at this new god; yet I predict
that soon he will be a living force in Greece.

Pentheus, there are two powers to bear in mind:
Demeter, the earth-goddess, who gives mankind
our daily bread; and Bacchus, Semele's son,
who gives us wine and thus oblivion,
banishing grief in sleep. There is indeed
no other medicine for our miseries.
We pour this god out in propitiation,
receiving absolution from the gods;
and this is the god you ridicule, denying
that he was sewn up in the thigh of Zeus.
I'll tell you a true story, listen to me:
when Zeus saved Dionysus from the lightning
and took the new-born child up to Olympus
Hera wished to get rid of it; but Zeus
devised a god-like scheme to circumvent her.
He took a little cloud from the blue sky
and shaped it like a child, which he presented
to Hera, meanwhile sending out the *real*
child Dionysus to the mountain nymphs,
to be raised as *his own son on the sly* by them.
The rumours started, the words got confused;
soon it was '*sewn up in the thigh*' of Zeus.
It's true; and this god is an oracle,
the Bacchic ecstasy oracular;
those so possessed can see into the future.
Strangely too, he has been known to play
a part in war by panicking whole armies
before they take their weapons in their hands.
The day is not far off when we shall see him
leaping by torchlight on the rocks of Delphi,
shaking the thyrsus, famous throughout Greece.
Pentheus, listen to me. You think coercion
can order humankind? How wrong you are!
Don't be so confident in your opinions;
receive this god in Thebes, pour out libations,
honour his rites and wear his ivy wreath.
Dionysus is not seducing women,
their conduct has its source in their own natures;
the chaste remain chaste, the unchaste unchaste.
Think of the satisfaction you derive

when people cheer you at the city gates;
similarly, I suspect, the god craves honour.
I certainly, and Cadmus, whom you mock,
will wear the ivy wreath and join the trance —
old men, perhaps, but not too old to dance.
Your words will not make *me* resist the gods.
I fear, in fact, for your own sanity.
What sort of medicine you're in need of, though,
to cure your sick condition, *I* don't know.

CHORUS

Tiresias, your wisdom is proverbial.
Whilst offering no insult to Apollo
you give due praise to the god Dionysus.

CADMUS
(*to* PENTHEUS)

Tiresias gives you sound advice, my boy.
Respect the pious traditions *we* respect.
You're not thinking straight; the rationalism
you prize so much has led you from the truth.
Even if, as you insist, this is no god
(and, sure, *I* don't know whether he is or not),
pretend he is, be gracious, that the house
of Semele receive honour for having borne him.
Don't forget Autonoë's son Actaeon, torn to bits
by his own hounds for boasting he could hunt
better than Artemis in her own country.
I don't want something like that to happen to you
so I'm going to wreathe your head with ivy. Here —
come with us, Pentheus, and honour the god!

PENTHEUS

Don't touch me! Go make idiots of yourselves
if you insist, but leave me out of it.
I intend to take strong measures against this man
who has filled your heads with his vicious rubbish.
(*to* SOLDIERS)
One of you go straight to his sanctuary
and wreck it, fling his 'holy' things around,

expose the whole place to the mountain wind —
this act will get to him like nothing else.
The rest, go search the city and seek out
this foreigner who drives our women mad
and fouls the country with his lechery;
and when you've found him bring him here to me.
I pronounce death by stoning; he'll regret
he brought to *Thebes* his Dionysian rite!

Exit PENTHEUS *to palace,* SOLDIERS *to wings.*

TIRESIAS

Young fool! He doesn't know what it is he's doing!
He was always a wilful boy, but now he's mad!
Cadmus, let's go and pray for the young king,
mad though he be, and for the city of Thebes,
and ask the god to take a lenient view.
Don't forget your thyrsus; here, lend me a hand,
let's put an arm around each others' shoulders;
it wouldn't do for two old men to fall!
We'll go and pay our dues to Dionysus.
God grant young Pentheus does nothing foolish
to bring down sorrow on your noble house.
I speak not as a prophet but as a friend:
that boy, seemingly sane, is round the bend.

Exeunt CADMUS *and* TIRESIAS.

CHORUS

Did you hear what Pentheus said?
Did you hear his blasphemy?
Did you hear him mock the god,
the son of Semele? — He
who, when the feast is laid,
is placed at the table-head;
whose gift is the holy dance,
the flute's exuberance,
the exhilaration of wine
when the gods sit down to dine,
the relief it gives to men

21

whose lives are filled with pain
when in the ivy glades
they lay exhausted heads.

Music and dance.

The harsh unthinking tongue
will lead to wretchedness
but the house of a wise man
survives storm and stress.
The gods in the blue sky
watch us night and day.
Wisdom is not of the mind,
we cannot think so far;
pride rushes life to its end,
and the proud ones who aspire
beyond human limitation
forfeit their own salvation —
a clinical psychosis.
The vain man always loses.

Music and dance.

Oh, to be on white
Aphrodite's isle
where love enchants the night
for a brief mortal while
and a thousand rivers flow
into the sands below.
Oh, to be where the airy
slopes of Olympus sweep
down to Pieria where
the nine Muses sleep.
Take us there, Dionysus,
where ecstasy isn't banned
and the holy thyrsus
sprouts from every hand!

Music and dance.

Our god, Semele's son,
delights in life-giving peace;
delights also in wine
which gives pain its release.
He hates those who refuse
the pleasures of this life,
long nights and quiet days.
Better to stand aloof
from pride-infected men
whose *hubris* wounds the gods;
common sense is enough
to live the life divine.
Raise your ivy rods;
praise the god of wine!

Music and dance; then SOLDIERS *bring in* DIONYSUS.
Enter PENTHEUS *from the palace.*

SOLDIER

King Pentheus, we've caught the man you wanted.
The beast was tame, made no move to escape,
gave himself up and didn't even turn pale
but kept his rosy complexion, smiling, saying
to tie his hands and bring him in to you.
I must admit I felt a bit put out.
'Sorry,' I said, 'I'm just obeying orders.'
He laughed as if he'd heard that line before.
However, sir, the imprisoned Bacchic women
escaped somehow and are running wild once more,
calling upon the name of Dionysus.
It was miraculous; their chains fell off,
the doors unlocked themselves and opened wide.
I fear this man is really a magician;
but here he is, in line with your instructions.

PENTHEUS

Untie his hands, we have him where we want him;
he's not so quick that he'll escape me now.
You're quite good-looking, friend; a definite advantage
for one whose task is the pursuit of women —

the aim, I take it, of your presence here.
The long hair tells me you're no fighting man,
cascading fondly down your baby face.
Your skin is soft, unhardened by the sun;
no doubt the women like your boyishness.
But tell me who you are. What is your race?

DIONYSUS

No secret about that. Perhaps you know
of Tmolus' flowery mountain capped with snow?

PENTHEUS

The Lydian mountain? Yes, I've heard of it.

DIONYSUS

I am as Greek as you; here I first saw the light.

PENTHEUS

Why do you bring these rituals back to Greece?

DIONYSUS

My guide is your own cousin Dionysus, son of Zeus.

PENTHEUS

Have you some god-creating *Lydian* Zeus?

DIONYSUS

I mean the Zeus here who knew Semele.

PENTHEUS

He instructed you in a dream, or face to face?

DIONYSUS

Face to face, and taught me his holy rites.

PENTHEUS

Tell me the nature of these curious sights.

DIONYSUS

A secret to the uninitiate.

PENTHEUS
And to the initiate, what benefit?

DIONYSUS
That is for me to know, you to find out.

PENTHEUS
You're trying to make me curious, answering me like that.

DIONYSUS
No, but our mysteries deplore impiety.

PENTHEUS
You spoke with Zeus; can you describe him to me?

DIONYSUS
He took the form he thought appropriate.

PENTHEUS
Oh, come now, you can do better than that!

DIONYSUS
I won't impart my privileged information to the mad.

PENTHEUS
Thebes is the first place you have brought your god?

DIONYSUS
All Asia dances in his celebration.

PENTHEUS
Of course, they're not up to *our* level of civilization.

DIONYSUS
Superior, though, in *this* respect, I'd say.

PENTHEUS
Do you do your mysteries by night or day?

DIONYSUS

Night mostly; dark creates a religious atmosphere.

PENTHEUS

And makes women do things indecent and impure.

DIONYSUS

Daylight has never interfered with licence.

PENTHEUS

You know you must be punished for your insolence?

DIONYSUS

And you for your impiety and ignorance.

PENTHEUS

Never lost for an answer. A fighter, with words at least!

DIONYSUS

Pronounce my sentence now; tell me the worst.

PENTHEUS

I'll start by shearing off those ringlets there.

> *He draws his sword; the* CHORUS *starts humming and drumming, softly and ominously;* PENTHEUS *does not fulfil his threat.*

DIONYSUS

I grow them for the god; it is holy hair.

PENTHEUS

Give me the wand you hold there in your hand.

DIONYSUS

It is not mine, but Dionysus' wand.

PENTHEUS
(sheathes his sword)
I'm afraid we must detain you here by force.

DIONYSUS

Dionysus will release me in due course.

PENTHEUS

Oh yes, when your Bacchants cry to him in grief.

SOLDIERS *silence the* CHORUS.

DIONYSUS

He is present now, watching over my life.

PENTHEUS

Oh really, where? I'm damned if I can see him.

DIONYSUS

Right here; you're blinded by your scepticism.

PENTHEUS

Bind him; he mocks me and the body politic.

DIONYSUS

Don't bind me; I'm the sane one, you the sick.

PENTHEUS

Bind him, I say; I have the greater power.

The SOLDIERS *are uncertain and do not bind him.*

DIONYSUS
(*laughs*)

You don't know what you're doing, or even who you are.

PENTHEUS
(*angrily*)

I am Pentheus, son of Agave and Echion.

DIONYSUS

'Pentheus' means 'sorrow'; so much the worse, old son.

PENTHEUS

Take him out of my sight and shut him up
where he can have his visions in the dark
and dance his dances. As for your lady friends,
                    (*indicates* CHORUS)
any more insolence and I'll have them sold
as slaves, or set their fingers to the looms,
so silencing the noise of their damned drums.

DIONYSUS

Right, lock me up, since it is so ordained.
I warn you, though, the god whom you offend
will wreak grave vengeance for this infamy;
you're locking *him* up when you lock up *me*.

SOLDIERS *remove* DIONYSUS, *followed by* PENTHEUS.

CHORUS

The king is in a rage,
his fury plain to see;
of mortal lineage,
he mocks a deity!
Us too he will soon bind
as servants of the god
who even now lies chained
in Pentheus' dark abode.

Or perhaps he's slipped his bonds
to dance with Maenads now
waving their ivy wands
under Olympus' brow
where Orpheus once charmed
birds out of the air
and in the glens, unharmed,
played upon the lyre
to the wild beasts there.

Son of Zeus, do you hear?
Pentheus' iron rod
will soon be drawing near.

Save us, immortal god;
come with your magic wand
and strike this murderous prince.
Save us, Dionysus, and
contain his violence!

DIONYSUS
(*shouts from inside the palace in a deep, resonant voice*)
Women of Asia, do you know my voice?

CHORUS
Listen, it's Dionysus calling us!

DIONYSUS
(*off*)
I speak to you as the son of Semele and Zeus!

CHORUS
Lord, lord, come from your prison-house!

DIONYSUS
(*off*)
Earth-tremor, shake the city to its base!

The palace shakes. There is a fall of masonry within, and a cloud of dust.

CHORUS
(*screaming with fear*)
Look, the earth trembles when he tells it to!

Our lord is in the palace; what shall we do?

Worship him; look, the palace quakes at his voice!

The stones crumble, crashing around the place!

The flame on Semele's tomb grows longer and brighter.

DIONYSUS
(*off*)
Let it blaze forth, the flame from the lightning-flash;
let fire run riot within Pentheus' house!

The sky reddens behind the palace.

CHORUS
Look, do you see the flame on Semele's tomb,
the flame lit when the lightning struck her womb?

More falling masonry.

Get down, Bacchae, throw yourselves on your faces
and worship Dionysus, destroyer of palaces!

DIONYSUS *appears before the palace in a cloud of smoke;*
Semele's flame subsides.

DIONYSUS
(*blithely*)
Women of Asia, why do you cringe like this?
Did you not hear the voice of Dionysus?
Get up and quit your trembling; shame on your cowardice!

CHORUS
What a relief it is to see your face!
We were alone, abandoned; now we rejoice!

DIONYSUS
Were you despondent when they took me out
to Pentheus' stinking prison-house like that?

CHORUS
Of course; we had no protection with you gone.
But tell us how you escaped from the impious man.

DIONYSUS
I simply tip-toed out without a sound.

But how? Did Pentheus not have you bound?

DIONYSUS
So he believed, but it was all in his head.
He took me round the back to a kind of shed
where, in the dark, we came upon a bull
he tied up, thinking it was me, the fool.
He bound its knees and hooves, sweat pouring off,
while I sat in a corner, trying not to laugh.
Then, when the earthquake happened and the flame
shot up over there upon Semele's tomb,
he imagined the whole place must be ablaze,
ran madly everywhere in a kind of daze
shouting for water. Then, thinking I'd gone,
he dashed into the courtyard; whereupon
materialized a sort of Dionysian ghost
provocatively in a thick cloud of dust.
Pentheus drew his sword and went half crazy,
lunging at thin air as if murdering *me*.
The rest you know: a heap of broken stone.
Pentheus is demented with exhaustion,
a man who raised his hand against a god.
I strolled out in my usual debonair mode
to reassure you. But I hear a click
of boots in the ruins; he'll be here in a tick.
Whatever he says, I mean to keep my cool;
a wise man exercises self-control.

Enter PENTHEUS *distraught, and* SOLDIERS.

PENTHEUS
This is too much, my prisoner's got loose;
just now I had him chained in an out-house.
                (*sees* DIONYSUS)
Oh, *there* you are! What's going on? How dare
you show your face before my very door?

DIONYSUS
Relax, control yourself, try not to shout.

31

PENTHEUS

I had you chained there; how did you get out?

DIONYSUS

Didn't I tell you I would be freed soon?

PENTHEUS

Did you? I hardly know what's going on.

DIONYSUS

I was freed by Dionysus, the god of wine.

PENTHEUS

Oh yes, the god of infamy, *that* one.

DIONYSUS

The god I represent is honoured by your disdain.

PENTHEUS
(*exasperated*)

Where *is* this 'god' whose name we hear again and again?

DIONYSUS

Not far; but he won't be easy to pin down.

PENTHEUS
(*to* SOLDIERS)

Go round the city and block every road.

DIONYSUS

Do you think mere road-blocks can contain a god?

Enter HERDSMAN.

PENTHEUS

You know everything, don't you, except what you ought to
    know.

DIONYSUS

I know the most important things, old boy.

But let's hear what this herdsman has to say;
obviously he wants to speak to you.
Don't worry, I'm not going to run away.

HERDSMAN
(*to* PENTHEUS)
Pentheus, King of Thebes, I come from Mount Cithaeron
(*points*)
where dazzling snow-drifts shine throughout the year.

PENTHEUS
(*superciliously*)
Really? And what great tidings bring you here?

HERDSMAN
I've seen the Bacchae in the hills above —
naked, my lord, and frantic; and I've come
to tell you of their fearsome goings-on,
things you'd hardly believe. May I be frank
or should I choose my words with care? I fear
your royal wrath should I speak out of turn.

PENTHEUS
Don't worry, friend, you can be frank with me;
the *innocent* don't suffer at my hands.
The more terrible your description of these rites,
however, the more severely will I punish
(*indicates*)
this man here who has driven our women mad.

HERDSMAN
First thing this morning, when the sun was up,
I drove my cattle to the high pastures
and there made out three companies of women,
one led by Agave, your own mother,
one by Ino, one by Autonoë.
They slept there peacefully, relaxed, on beds
of pine-needles and oak-leaves,
as if they'd simply curled up on the ground —
modestly, though; not like the women drunk

33

with strong wine and flute music, mad for love
in the solitude of the woods, that we'd been told of.
Agave, when she heard the cattle moving,
woke and stood up among the Bacchae there,
calling to *them* to wake up, which they did,
rubbing the drowsy slumber from their eyes
and getting to their feet. A lovely sight —
young wives and matrons, fresh unmarried girls,
lined up beneath the pines, tossing their curls,
tugging their fawnskins, fastening them with snakes
whose tongues flickered around their rosy cheeks.
Young mothers, those with children newly born
so that their breasts were full, suckled gazelles
or lambs, their children being left at home.
They put on wreaths of ivy, briony, oak,
and one, taking a thyrsus, struck a rock
from which a cold spring of clear water leapt.
Another drove her stick into the earth
from which there sprang a fountain of red wine;
while those who wanted milk had only to scratch
the soil with their finger-nails and the milk flowed.
Honey dripped from the tips of their fennel wands.
Had you been there to see it you'd pronounce
devotion to the god you now denounce.
We cow-herds and the shepherds got together
to talk about the amazing things we'd seen,
each story more amazing than another.
One man who knows the town and, for that reason,
thinks himself pretty smart, had an idea:
'Why don't we mountain men capture Agave,
Pentheus' mother, just to please the king?'
It *seemed* a good idea. We went and hid
in the undergrowth; then, in a little while,
the women waved their wands and started dancing,
calling upon the name of Dionysus.
The *mountain* seemed to dance, the *animals* danced,
the rocks and bushes, *everything* was dancing.
I spied your mother, left my hiding-place
and made a grab at her, but she cried out:
'O Maenads mine, these men are stalking us;

each of you take your wand and stand by me!'
We lit out pretty quick, you can imagine,
and so escaped death by dismemberment.
They saw the cattle grazing, though, and went
for the poor creatures with their bare hands.
One flung a frightened heifer to the ground,
some seized the cows and tore them limb from limb.
The air was filled with ribs and broken legs;
flesh dripped from the pine-branches; furious bulls
were tripped and pinioned there by delicate girls
who stripped them faster than your royal eyes
could blink; that done, skimming along like birds,
they scoured the plain around Asopus' river,
invaded Hysiae and Erythrae,
two townlands in the foot-hills of Cithaeron,
and wrecked them both; snatched babies from their cradles.
Oddly, whatever they plundered, bronze or iron,
stayed on their shoulders as if balanced there.
Each head blazed, but the hair was not consumed.
The men, of course, enraged by this invasion,
took up arms in resistance and confusion;
but then, my lord, a curious thing occurred.
The spears they threw seemed to inflict no wound.
The Bacchae, flinging the thyrsus like a spear,
inflicted *grievous* wounds. Women routed the men!
There was a god there! Anyhow, the Bacchae
returned to their favourite place among the mountains
where Bacchus made the wine-and-water fountains;
and snakes licked the dried blood from their cheeks.
Pentheus, whoever this strange god may be,
receive him here in Thebes; his powers are great.
He gave us wine, my lord, he gave us love;
no other god has showered such benefits from above.

CHORUS

At the risk of Pentheus' rage it must be said,
than Dionysus there is no greater god.

PENTHEUS

This Bacchism, spreading like a forest fire,

35

makes us ridiculous. We must prepare.
Soldiers, go quickly to the Northern Gate.
Order shield-bearing units, horse and foot,
bowmen and armourers, to meet me there
and go subdue the Maenads. This is war!

Exeunt SOLDIERS *and* HERDSMAN.

DIONYSUS

Pentheus, you refuse to listen to my advice;
and yet, despite your stupid wickedness,
I warn you not to provoke Dionysus
or hunt his Bacchae from their holy place.

PENTHEUS

Shut up. You broke your chains, now be content;
or must I think up some new punishment?

DIONYSUS

If I were you I'd make a sacrifice
to Dionysus, not fly in his face.
A mortal, you declare war on a god?

PENTHEUS

Oh yes, a sacrifice — of women's blood!

DIONYSUS

Your soldiers will be put to flight, their bronze
shields routed by the women's fennel wands.

PENTHEUS

You're getting on my nerves, do you know that?
Jailed or at loose, your mouth is never shut.

He makes to exit.

DIONYSUS

Wait a minute . . . I think I've hit on a solution.

PENTHEUS
(*pauses, sarcastically*)
Oh yes? Do I proclaim a Bacchic revolution?

DIONYSUS
I'll get the women back, and without force.

PENTHEUS
Indeed? You're up to some new game, of course.

DIONYSUS
I'm trying to save your *life*, you pompous twit!

PENTHEUS
A trick to keep alive the Bacchic rite.

DIONYSUS
A scheme I have devised with the god they love.

PENTHEUS
Where is my sword? I think I've heard enough.

DIONYSUS
(*mischievously*)
Would you like to see what the Bacchae *do* in the wood?

PENTHEUS
(*a thoughtful and embarrassed pause*)
Well, now you mention it, I suppose I should.
I'd give a *lot* to see them if I could.

DIONYSUS
(*laughs*)
Why are you suddenly so curious?

PENTHEUS
I couldn't bear to see them *drunk*, of course.

DIONYSUS
You want to *see* them, though, am I not right?

PENTHEUS

If I could hide in the bushes, out of sight.

DIONYSUS

They'll sniff you out, however low you lie.

PENTHEUS

Well, in that case, let's go there openly.

DIONYSUS

Shall we start now? It's not so very far.

PENTHEUS

All right, let's go; I'm ready when you are.

DIONYSUS

First you must dress up in a linen gown.

PENTHEUS

A linen gown? I can't go as a man?

DIONYSUS

Go as a man there and they'll do you in.

PENTHEUS

You're up to all the tricks; you think of everything.

DIONYSUS

The great god Dionysus taught me those.

PENTHEUS
(giggles)

How shall I change my sex as you propose?

DIONYSUS

Come on inside and we'll find something nice.

PENTHEUS

But, women's clothes? I couldn't show my face!

DIONYSUS
Look, do you want to do this thing or not?

PENTHEUS
(*shyly*)
Of course; but what disguise should I adopt?

DIONYSUS
We must do something first about your hair.

PENTHEUS
Yes, and what sort of costume should I wear?

DIONYSUS
A linen gown, your head in a silk scarf.

PENTHEUS
Anything else you think I ought to have?

DIONYSUS
A dappled fawnskin; in your hand a thyrsus.

PENTHEUS
I can't do it; it's too ridiculous.

DIONYSUS
Declare war on the Bacchae and you'll die.

PENTHEUS
Then I must go and watch them like a spy.

DIONYSUS
A show of force and the women won't be pleased.

PENTHEUS
How can I get through Thebes unrecognized?

DIONYSUS
Leave it to me; we'll go by a back route.

PENTHEUS

No-one must recognize me in the street.

DIONYSUS

There, there; come inside and we'll kit you out.

PENTHEUS

I need to think. Do I ride out with my men
or do I sneak up in a linen gown?

PENTHEUS *goes into the palace.*

DIONYSUS

This idiot is walking into a trap;
he will visit the Bacchae and will surely die.
He will be punished with insanity.
Indeed, he's mad already; a sane Pentheus
would never dream of dressing like a woman.
I want to see the people laugh at him
in his long gown among the streets of Thebes —
a fine humiliation. I must choose
the very clothes in which he meets his death,
struck down by his own mother Agave.
He will know soon enough that Dionysus
is a *real* god, truly the son of Zeus,
kindly and strict, both, to the human race.

DIONYSUS *follows* PENTHEUS *into the palace.*

ACT TWO

The same; afternoon. Enter the CHORUS *as before. Music and dance.*

CHORUS

Oh, for Dionysian night
and the white ghosts of feet
dancing in the bright
dew, magical and sweet!
Oh, for the fun of a fawn
in the clear meadow-light
who breaks cover to run
without fear, without fright,
to river and forest where
no man has ever gone
and crouches there alone!

What pleases best, what grand
gift can the gods bestow
more than the conquering hand
over the fallen foe?
It's still the same old story,
a fight for love and glory,
and every heart admits that this is so.

Gods move at their own pace
ignoring earthly hours;
when proud minds race
in search of godly powers,
the gods provide correction
to the vain man who tries
to replace faith with action,

tradition with vanities.
Truth as old as the hills,
derived from very nature,
rules the world and rules
the life of every creature.

What pleases best, what grand
gift can the gods bestow
more than the conquering hand
over the fallen foe?
It's still the same old story,
a fight for love and glory,
and every heart admits that this is so.

Music and dance.

Happy the man who escapes from the whistling sea
and finds a berth beside the protective quay;
happy the man who rises above despair
and makes his way to fortune or to power.
A thousand hopes inspire a thousand men.
Some make it, though again
others will fail. No matter, peace of mind
is the greatest gift the gods grant to mankind.

Enter DIONYSUS *from the palace, calling back to*
PENTHEUS.

DIONYSUS
Come on, old sport, with your lascivious eyes;
come on out, Pentheus, in your fineries;
come on, you ruffian, so quick to snoop
on your own mother and her Bacchic troop!

Enter PENTHEUS *from the palace, dressed in a woman's*
clothes, so that DIONYSUS *laughs.* PENTHEUS *is bemused*
and obedient to DIONYSUS.

PENTHEUS
I seem to see two suns in the blue skies,

a double Thebes. What's happened to my eyes?

> DIONYSUS *takes* PENTHEUS *by the hand and leads him*
> *downstage.*

You seem to be a bull leading me now;
a pair of horns has grown out of your brow.
                    (*but there are no horns*)

DIONYSUS
The modish god has given us our due —
horns for myself, a linen gown for you.

PENTHEUS
(*poses*)
How do I look, like Ino or Autonoë?
Do I stand like my own mother, gracefully?

DIONYSUS
Yes, you're her very image, to be sure.
Hold on, a curl has slipped from your coiffure.

PENTHEUS
I must have shaken it from its proper place
while practising my Bacchic ecstasy.

DIONYSUS
That's better; but your girdle has come loose
and your gown isn't as straight as it might be.

PENTHEUS
It's longer on the left than on the right;
look at it from behind and make it straight.

DIONYSUS
(*ironically*)
Remember this above when you discover
how modest the mad Maenads really *are*.

PENTHEUS

How does a Bacchant hold her ivy wand?
In the right hand, like this, or the left hand?

DIONYSUS

In the right hand, and shake it on the beat.
Don't worry, you'll soon get the hang of it.

PENTHEUS
(*wistfully*)
If only I could overturn Cithaeron
with my bare hands, my shoulder to the stone!

DIONYSUS
(*severely*)
You mustn't interfere with the Bacchic shrines.
Do as I say and hide among the pines.

PENTHEUS

I see them there like birds in a dark grove,
all snuggled up in the warm nests of love!

DIONYSUS
(*laughs*)
That's what you *want* to see; be careful, though,
that those you spy upon don't see you too.

PENTHEUS

Let's saunter through the city; I'm the one,
of all men, after all, who dares do this alone.

DIONYSUS

Alone you strike for stricken Thebes; and how
striking a destiny awaits you now!
Come on, I'll take you to the Maenads' glen;
somebody else will bring you home again.

PENTHEUS

Ah, that will be my mother carrying me!

DIONYSUS
Through Thebes you will be carried shoulder-high.

PENTHEUS
I admit I have a taste for pomp and ceremony.

DIONYSUS
Your mother's arms will bear you to the palace.

PENTHEUS
You're going to spoil me with your promises!

DIONYSUS
Yes, in a sense, I'll 'spoil' you; *they* will too.

PENTHEUS
The Bacchae? Still, I suppose it's no more than my due.

Exit PENTHEUS *to wings.*

DIONYSUS
Truly, what an amazing man he is!
His death will be amazing too, a death
to be spoken of with awe in times to come.
Agave, Ino and Autonoë, Cadmus'
daughters, reach out your hands to Pentheus
who declares war on you; though you shall win.

DIONYSUS *follows* PENTHEUS.

CHORUS
O hounds of madness, race to Mount Cithaeron
where Cadmus' daughters dance with wild abandon
and madden them, like hounds hot on the chase,
against this fool got up in Bacchic dress!
His mother will be the first to spot the man
crouching on some high rock behind a pine
and call to the Bacchae, shouting: 'Who is this
stranger upon our mountain, spying on us?
Who is his mother? No, he had no mother,

he was borne by some Egyptian witch or other.'

> Justice, play your part,
> your sword pierce the heart
> of Echion's wicked son,
> a mere mortal man
> who arrogantly flies
> to Bacchic mysteries,
> confused, demented, mad,
> to combat with a god
> only death can decide.

> *Shouting and dancing.*

> *Now*, Dionysus, *now,*
> like a bull or a roaring lion
> furious of brow,
> kill the son of Echion!
> Descend upon the spy
> and fling the man sky-high;
> crack his mortal bones
> upon Cithaeron's stones:
> *that* is his destiny.

> *Music and dance, then enter a* SOLDIER.

SOLDIER
(*falls to his knees and weeps*)
O house of Cadmus, how I mourn for your disgrace,
respected once the length and breadth of Greece!

CHORUS
You've come from Mount Cithaeron; what news do you bring?

SOLDIER
News of the death of Pentheus my king.

CHORUS
(*music and dance*)
Pipe and drum, pipe and drum;

let Thebes know Dionysus, the lord of the dance, is come!

SOLDIER

What's going on? How dare you so exult
when death has overcome King Pentheus?

CHORUS

We are foreigners and belong to a foreign cult;
besides, imprisonment holds no further dread for us.

SOLDIER
(*rises*)

Do you think there's no-one fit to take his place?

CHORUS

Not Thebes but Dionysus governs *us*.

SOLDIER

I don't quite understand you; but to sing
at such misfortune is a shameful thing.

CHORUS
(*avidly*)

Tell us the details; how did Pentheus die?
And why are you so well informed about it?

SOLDIER

I went there as a look-out, with the young
(*distastefully*)
'Lydian chap' who acted as our guide.
Once we had left the outskirts of the city
and crossed the Asopus, we began to climb
up Mount Cithaeron, where the Bacchae live.
We stopped in a glade, keeping our voices down,
so we might see without ourselves being seen.
There was a gorge below us ringed with crags
and bubbling with spring-water. There, in the shade
of pines, the Maenads sat, engaged in tasks —
twining an undone wand with ivy-leaves
or practising their Bacchic hymns together.

47

The ill-fated Pentheus couldn't see them clearly.
'Soldier,' said he, 'you know, from where we stand
I can't make out the Bacchic worshippers;
but if I climbed a pine there on the cliff
I'd have a good view of their shameful rites.'
So then the Lydian fellow did a most
amazing thing; he grasped a mountain pine
with his bare hands and bent the whole thing down
until it touched the earth like a drawn bow —
miraculous really, when you think of it.
He seated Pentheus on the topmost branch
and let the tree spring from his hands upright,
but gently, so that Pentheus held on tight.
He saw the Bacchae, but they saw him too.
In fact, he was just springing into view
when Dionysus spoke out of the blue,
the stranger having vanished: 'Women, here
is the man who made a mockery of you,
of me, my mysteries; now punish him.'
Suddenly, at these words, a blaze of fire
rose between earth and heaven, the air was still
and the glade oddly silent; nothing stirred.
The Bacchic women hadn't clearly heard
the god's pronouncement, but they stood and stared.
Once more he roared aloud his vengeful word
and Cadmus' daughters, all the Bacchae too,
flew like doves into the watery glen
with its harsh rocks, inspired by the wild god.
And when they spied the king, perched on a pine,
they climbed a cliff and started stoning him,
while others flung the thyrsus like a spear
at Pentheus, although they struck the air;
for Pentheus was perched too high for them,
poor man, alone in his exposure there.
They tore the branches from an oak and tried
to dig the pine up, but that didn't work;
but then, Agave, his own mother, cried,
'Stand in a circle round the tree itself,
uproot it, throw the spy from the high branches
lest he disclose the secret of our dances!'

48

A thousand hands took hold of the pine-tree
and tore it from the earth; so Pentheus fell
with a great scream, knowing the end was nigh.
Agave was the first to go for him.
He flung his veil and hair aside and cried,
'Mother, I am your own son Pentheus;
you won't, for God's sake, kill your only child?'
Agave, foaming at the mouth, eyes wild
in her head, was clearly not in her right mind.
Maddened by Dionysus, she took hold
of Pentheus' left arm, her foot upon his chest,
and tore it from the shoulder with a strength
not hers but given her by the Bacchic god.
Ino, meanwhile, was tearing at his breast,
Autonoë, the whole Dionysian horde.
A frightful scream arose and Pentheus moaned
while life remained to him, the women loud
with triumph. Someone carried off an arm,
someone a foot, the sandal laced to it.
The women stripped the ribs and, smeared with blood,
played 'catch' with raw pieces of Pentheus' flesh.
His body lies dispersed among the rocks
and glades of Mount Cithaeron, hard to find.
His mother stuck his head upon her thyrsus,
believing it to be a lion's head.
She's left the mountain and returned to town
acclaiming Dionysus as her lord;
though bitter tears will be her true reward.
I'm leaving here; I cannot face the scene
when Cadmus' favourite daughter returns with her dead son.
A sound and simple heart is all I have —
our best possession this side of the grave.

Exit.

CHORUS
Dance and render praise;
King Pentheus is gone
who went out in disguise
to spy on the Bacchic throng.

When Dionysus led
the imposter to their glade
what triumph then was theirs!
But here comes Agave,
exultant, her fine eyes
flashing in her head.
Make way for her, make way!

Enter AGAVE *from the wings, panting, mad, with
Pentheus' head in her hands. Other* BACCHAE *line up at
the sides of the stage, where they remain to the end of
the play.* AGAVE *holds up Pentheus' head, from which
the* CHORUS *shrink.*

AGAVE

Women of Asia, Dionysian maids,
I bring you from the mountain-sides
a vine-branch newly cut;
I bring you from Cithaeron
the head of a young lion,
the fruit of our pursuit.

CHORUS
(*shocked but conniving*)
We see it and share your pride.
Who tore away the head?

AGAVE

I did, and heard them cry,
'More power to Agave!'

CHORUS

And Cadmus' other daughters
took part in the slaughter?

AGAVE

Autonoë and Ino
tore at the ravening beast,
a mad mountain lion;
come and join the feast!

CHORUS

A feast, you wretched woman?

AGAVE

(*strokes Pentheus' head*)

Look, it's almost human —
a young one; see how close
the new-sprung hair grows,
and under the strong chin
I see the beard begin.

CHORUS

True, its unruly thatch
gives it a bestial air.

AGAVE

What do you think of my catch?

CHORUS

A head fine and fair.

AGAVE

The people of Thebes will cheer.

CHORUS

(*ironically*)

And Pentheus beside?

AGAVE

Will be proud of his mother.

CHORUS

(*harshly*)

Now are you satisfied?

AGAVE

Satisfied? I'm *delirious*
at the fine thing I've done!

CHORUS
(*sorrowfully*)
So show the rest of us
the great prize you've won.

AGAVE
(*shows the head to the audience; evening now*)
People of Thebes, I want you to see this prize,
the lion Cadmus' daughters caught and killed —
not with nets and spears, but with our own bare hands.
Where were your huntsmen and your armourers
when we alone, my two sisters and I,
put paid to the murderous creature and tore it limb from limb?
Where are my father Cadmus and Pentheus my son?
He will hang this in the palace hall in honour of what I've done!

Enter CADMUS *and* SOLDIERS *bearing the remains of*
PENTHEUS *on a litter, covered with a sheet.*

CADMUS
Bring in the remains of Pentheus; set him down.
God knows, I searched for him in wood and glen,
picking the pieces up and gathering them
to make sense of the body. I'd already
returned with old Tiresias from the dance
when I was told about the frightful deed
my daughters did. So I went back, and now
return my grandson, whom the Maenads killed.
Autonoë and Ino were still there,
insane beyond belief; I had them taken
to Aristaeus' house while poor Agave
was gaily dancing her way back to Thebes —
and there she is indeed, a grievous sight.

AGAVE
Father, be proud, for you have truly sired
the finest daughters of whom Thebes can boast —
Ino, Autonoë, and myself the most,
who left the loom for better things, to hunt
wild beasts. Look, here in my hands I bear

52

one of the noblest trophies that there are,
a lion's head for Pentheus' dining hall!
Here, father, take it; invite everyone
to a great feast in honour of what I've done!

CADMUS
(*refuses the head*)
Oh, what a dreadful sight; a sight to blind the eyes!
A sanguinary act performed by wretched hands!
What a fine sacrifice you give the gods,
summoning Thebes, and me, to a noble feast!
What a dire moment, this, for both of us.
Dionysus, though provoked, has been too harsh;
Semele's son has ruined his own house!

AGAVE
What a cantankerous old man you are.
What a bad temper, father; what black looks!
I wish my son were a hunter like his mother,
hot in the chase with the young men of Thebes;
his interest, though, lies only in fighting gods.
It's time you spoke to him about it, father.
Somebody go and fetch him here to me
so he can take part in our celebrations!

CADMUS
If you could understand your own actions,
daughter, what rending heartbreak would be yours!
If you remain insane, as you are now,
at least you won't know what it is you've done.

AGAVE
Why heartbreak? Why insane? What's going on?

CADMUS
(*holds her*)
Agave, stand here; look up at the sky.

AGAVE
I'm looking as you tell me to; but why?

CADMUS

Does it seem any clearer than before?

AGAVE

Darker but clearer; look, there's an evening star!

CADMUS

Do you think your *mind* is any clearer now?

AGAVE

I think so, yes; darker but clear, somehow.

CADMUS

Listen to me and try to *answer* clearly.

AGAVE

Yes . . . What were we talking about just now?

CADMUS

To whose house did you go as a young bride?

AGAVE

Echion's . . . Yes, Echion was my husband.

CADMUS

You had a son, remember? Who was he?

AGAVE

Pentheus was the son I bore Echion.

CADMUS

Whose head is that you're holding in your hands?

AGAVE

The women said it was a mountain lion.

CADMUS

Look at the face; you only have to glance.

AGAVE *looks, pauses and screams.*

AGAVE

Whose is this head? What am I holding here?

CADMUS

Look carefully and *everything* will be clear.

AGAVE

Oh no, no, no; it can't be true!

CADMUS

A lion's head; is that what it seems to you?

AGAVE

This is the head of my son Pentheus.

CADMUS

He is already mourned by the rest of us.

AGAVE
(*frantic*)
Who killed him? Why do I hold his head in my hands?

CADMUS

Oh God, that you should learn the truth of it!

AGAVE

Tell me before I die of misery!

CADMUS

Agave, you and your sisters murdered him.

AGAVE

We *murdered* him? Where? Here in the royal palace?

CADMUS

No, where Actaeon's hounds devoured Actaeon.

AGAVE

Cithaeron? What was Pentheus doing there?

CADMUS

He went to see what you and the rest were up to.

AGAVE

What on earth were *we* doing on Mount Cithaeron?

CADMUS

You were possessed; all Thebes was in a trance.

AGAVE
(*momentarily calm*)
I see now, Dionysus drove us mad.

CADMUS

We maddened *him*, failing to call him god.

AGAVE
(*grief-stricken*)
Where is the belovèd body of my son?

CADMUS

Here he is; it was I who brought him in.

AGAVE

I hope his fine body is in — one piece?

CADMUS

As best we could; and now we have the head.

AGAVE
(*angrily*)
And where lay *Pentheus'* guilt in this affair?

CADMUS

Like you, he refused reverence to a god;
and the same god has ruined all of us —
yourself, our family, the house of Thebes.
And I, Cadmus, with no son of my own,
must see, dear daughter, *your* belovèd son
horribly and grotesquely dead. Our house

(takes Pentheus' head)
looked up to you, my grandson. You maintained
my dynasty, the son of my own daughter.
All Thebes looked up to you, and no-one dared
speak ill of your old grandfather lest Pentheus
respond severely. Now I shall lose face —
I, Cadmus the Great, who founded Thebes,
and sowed the soldiers who protect us now.
No longer will you take my hand and say,
'Grandfather, who has wronged or angered you
that I may punish him?' I am disconsolate
and you, daughter, destined to endless grief;
your sisters too. If any man disdain
the gods, consider Pentheus' death and think again!

CHORUS
Pity for Cadmus! Pity for Cadmus' pain!

AGAVE
(sobs uncontrollably)
One day has wrecked my life, one day destroyed
my happiness and turned my pride to grief.
My one wish now is to lay out the corpse
for burial. Death can take me when he pleases.

CADMUS
Touch him no further now; your very hands
are those that murdered him, remember that.

AGAVE
What other hands should care for my dead son?
Can they do greater harm than they have done?

CADMUS
(relents)
Look lightly, gods, upon this impious act
or strike *me* if you must. Remove the sheet.

SOLDIERS *remove the sheet, revealing the body of*
PENTHEUS, *supine but in a contorted position, his*

clothes arranged to suggest dismemberment.

AGAVE
(*keens*)
O God in heaven, what a piteous sight!
And how unnatural these tears, my son,
which should be yours over my own dead face!
And now, father, the fine head let us place
where it belongs and fit, as best we can,
the body in one piece, formal and straight.

They do so.

Goodbye, dear child; I'm going to veil you now
with my own veil; forgive me. Which torn limb
shall I mourn most? This hand? Was that the first
to break when I dismembered my own son?
The wrist, the elbow . . . What a fine young man!
And these dead genitals that had no time
to ensure continuance of our royal line.
Cover him; Pentheus, my son, goodnight!
Take up the litter; have him lie in state,
(*angrily*)
ensnared in death by a vindictive fate.

The sky darkens; thunder and lightning; DIONYSUS, *in
an immense bull-mask reaching to his knees, enters
from the palace, his arms folded authoritatively.*

CHORUS
(*in awe*)
Dionysus stands in the palace door —
the very god we worship and adore!

DIONYSUS
(*in his resonant voice*)
Now know me as a god in my true form;
I come in lightning to my mother's tomb.

Thunder and lightning.

I come to the city of Thebes where I was *born*
in lightning, though you people slighted me,
discrediting my true divinity,
mocking my sacred rites — a grievous error
the royal house of Thebes will rue for ever.
King Pentheus, my cousin, was the worst in blasphemy,
denied my godhead and imprisoned me;
and so, at his own mother's hands, he died —
a harsh response, you will say, to a foolish deed.
Ah, but no god is mocked; our actions show
to men the obedience they must undergo.
Agave and her sisters must at once
leave Thebes; their exile is their proper penance.
Cadmus, for your equivocation, you
must follow your daughters into exile too
and change into a snake; though, for your love,
you shall sit down at last among the gods above.
                    (*to all*)
Remember, Dionysus, son of Zeus,
pronounces sentence on you. Had your choice
been the wise one, you would have lived to see
Thebes prosper in perpetuity,
favoured by Zeus my father; but oh, no!

CADMUS
Great god, be merciful; we didn't know.

DIONYSUS
Well, you know now; you should have known before.

CADMUS
I grant you; but your vengeance goes too far!

DIONYSUS
You *goaded* me too far; me, Dionysus!

CADMUS
Can't gods, unlike mere men, forego vindictiveness?

DIONYSUS

Everything was ordained by my father Zeus.

AGAVE

It's hopeless, Daddy; there can be no appeal.

DIONYSUS

Right, no appeal; so why postpone the inevitable?

CADMUS

Agave, dearest daughter, what misery for us —
you and your sisters, me and Pentheus.
I, at my age, to live so far from home!
Will there be any peace for us, even beyond the tomb?

AGAVE

(*embraces* CADMUS *tearfully*)
Dionysus will insist that we live apart.

CADMUS

Yes, I know; and the thought breaks my heart.

AGAVE

Oh Daddy, where on earth am I to go?

CADMUS

Athens? Heraklion? It's up to you.

AGAVE

Goodbye, Thebes! Goodbye, the land I love!
I leave you now, a wretched fugitive,
who lived here as a girl, a bride, an honoured spouse.

CADMUS

Daughter, go now to Aristaeus' house
where Ino and Autonoë prepare
to leave, like you, the land of Thebes for ever.

AGAVE

Oh Daddy, how I grieve for your grim fate!

CADMUS
Just as I grieve for yours, my favourite.

AGAVE
(*defiantly*)
There is much cruelty in a god who sheds
such misery upon mere mortal heads!

DIONYSUS
Such cruelty as I found at *Pentheus'* hand,
my name dishonoured here in my own land!

Exit DIONYSUS *in a puff of smoke.*

AGAVE
Goodbye, dear father; the gods keep you safe.

CADMUS
(*embracing her*)
Goodbye, my child; good fortune in this life!

Exit CADMUS.

AGAVE
Take me where my sisters are
at Aristaeus' house.
I mean to travel far
from that evil place
Cithaeron. I renounce
the Dionysian dance.
Take my wreath and rod;
let others serve the god!

She hands her wreath and thyrsus to the CHORUS;
exeunt all but the CHORUS. *Music and dance.*

CHORUS
Gods come in various shapes
and act in curious ways;
neither our fears nor hopes

work out as we suppose.
Life is unfair, no doubt,
and yet the gods demand
our homage, which is what
we've tried to demonstrate.

What pleases best, what grand
gift can the gods bestow
more than the conquering hand
over the fallen foe?
It's still the same old story,
a fight for love and glory,
and every heart admits that this is so.

Gods move at their own pace
ignoring earthly hours;
when proud minds race
in search of godly powers
the gods provide correction
to the vain man who tries
to replace faith with action,
tradition with vanities.
Truth as old as the hills,
derived from very nature,
rules the world and rules
the life of every creature.

(in unison)
What pleases best, what grand
gift can the gods bestow
more than the conquering hand
over the fallen foe?
It's still the same old story,
a fight for love and glory,
and every heart admits that this is so!

*Music and dance; thunder and lightning; triumphant
reappearance of* DIONYSUS, *his arms folded authoritatively.*